Baptism and Church Membership

James H. Waltner

FAITH AND LIFE PRESS
Newton, Kansas

MENNONITE PUBLISHING HOUSE
Scottdale, Pennsylvania

ISBN 0-87303-032-X

Copyright © 1979 by Faith and Life Press, Newton,
Kansas 67114 and Mennonite Publishing House,
Scottdale, Pennsylvania 15683

Printed in the United States of America

Foreword

Abram "built an altar to the Lord;" the psalmist sang "a new song;" Isaiah responded to a vision of God with "Here am I;" Jesus read from the Scriptures in the synagogue; early Christians are together "with glad and generous hearts, praising God." All of them worshiped, responding to the revelation of God.

That revelation is still real, enriched by almost two thousand years of adoration and by new insights that come every day. In Christian communities we feel drawn together to rejoice, share, and pray, as we respond to God's love in our generation.

This pamphlet is one of a series relating to the worship of the church. It is our hope that in creation and expression it will become more and more a work of the people. These booklets are therefore designed to be used by all who participate in the planning and leading of worship services, not only by pastors. May the presence of Christ be recognized as we continue together in His name.

Worship and Arts Committee
Orlando Schmidt, Chairperson

Contents

FOREWORD 3

INTRODUCTION 7

  I. THE BASIS FOR BAPTISM 8
    Baptism in the Bible 8
    How the Church Has Understood Baptism 11
    Anabaptist-Mennonite Practice and
      Understanding 13

 II. SUGGESTIONS FOR OUR PRACTICE
    OF BAPTISM 19
    Clarifying What We Say by Baptism . . . 19
    Preparing for Baptism and Church
      Membership 23
    Planning the Baptism Service 27
    Baptism Service Forms 30
    After Baptism 36

III. RELATED SERVICES 38
    Reception of Members by Letter and
      Affirmation of Faith 38
    Covenant Renewal 41
    Parent-Child Dedication 45

FOOTNOTES 48

APPENDIX A. Resources for Instruction . . 51

APPENDIX B. Readiness for Baptism and
    Church Membership Questionnaire . . . 53

BIBLIOGRAPHY 61

INTRODUCTION

"Lord, this year I'm going to do it!" read a young mother's diary entry for January 1. "It" was a commitment to Christ that culminated in baptism and joining the church. Later as she described the event, her eyes sparkled. She talked about the new freedom in commitment, and the joy of her new family in Christ.

Baptism is a "moment" in which a direction for life with Christ is confirmed in a public act. This booklet on baptism and church membership is written for pastors and church leaders. The focus will be on baptism as an act of uniting not only with Christ, but also with a congregation of Christ's people. The congregation is viewed here as an expression of the body of Christ, a part of the larger body of Christ's church. So as we speak of baptism we will also deal with issues of church membership.

Sources for this booklet include not only personal study and experience but also consultations with Mennonite pastors and counsel with church leaders in the Mennonite and the General Conference Mennonite Church. While there are many common practices in our congregations, there is also diversity. This is so with the understanding and practice of baptism. This booklet will not present the one and only way of baptism. Rather, it is written in the

7

hope that pastors and congregations will use it as a guide to study further and practice with greater integrity this important event in the life of believers and the congregation.

We begin by examining the biblical passages, the history of baptism in the church, and our own Anabaptist-Mennonite understandings. Suggestions will then be shared for the contemporary practice of baptism. Sample services and forms are included. Ideas are also shared for reception of members, covenant-renewal, and related services.

I. THE BASIS FOR BAPTISM

BAPTISM IN THE BIBLE

The word, *baptize*, "to wash" or "dip," appears seventy-six times in the New Testament. *Baptism* is used twenty-two times. A few passages use related forms of the word. Most references to *baptize* and *baptism* are in the Gospels and Acts. There are fifteen references in Paul's letters.

Jewish Baptism and John the Baptist The practice of baptism has its roots in Jewish baptism in which water was used for ritual cleansing. Proselytes to Judaism were baptized as an act of self-dedication to the God of Israel. The Exodus is the archetype of baptism. Crossing the Red Sea and the Jordan into the promised land was the symbolism behind Jewish baptism of proselytes. Proselytes were identifying themselves with Israel's history and heritage.

John the Baptist used this ritual, stationing himself at the Jordan. But he administered it to both Jews and Gentiles (Mark 1:5). He emphasized the ethical significance of the rite: "Bear fruit that befits repentance" (Matt. 3:8). He also linked baptism with his proclamation of the coming kingdom of God: "Repent, for the kingdom of heaven is at hand" (Matt. 3:2). John's baptism can be seen as a rite of moral purification designed to prepare persons for the coming kingdom of God. (The passages

8

referring to John's baptism are Matthew 3:1-17;
Mark 1:4-11; 11:27ff; Luke 3:3-20; John 1:19-33;
3:23ff; 10:40; Acts 1:5; 11:16; 13:24; 18:25; 19:4.)

Jesus' Baptism Jesus was baptized by John. Why was He baptized and what did His baptism mean? Through this act Jesus did several things:
1. He identified himself with His people.
2. He placed himself into the messianic movement.
3. He designated His work as a continuation of John's work.
4. He accepted God's mission for His life.[1]

In understanding Jesus' baptism as an ordination into God's mission, we recall the temptations that immediately followed (Matt. 4:1-11; Mark 1:12, 13; Luke 4:1-13). We also need to note the linking of the voice from heaven, "Thou art my beloved Son. . ." (Mark 1:11), with the allusion in the servant song of Isaiah 42:1, and with the voice at the transfiguration (Mark 9:7). From the transfiguration experience Jesus went to Jerusalem and the cross. In the baptism of Jesus the consciousness of divine sonship, of mission as a servant, and of crucifixion and death are related.

The Early Church From the day of Pentecost the early church practiced baptism as a symbol of entry into the Christian community (Acts 2:38, 41). Baptism was closely connected with repentance and with reception of the Holy Spirit. It followed on "hearing," "receiving the word," and "believing" (Acts 8:12; 16:14, 15). There are twenty-seven references to baptism in the Book of Acts.

Paul's letters give us the fullest New Testament exposition of the meaning of baptism. Key passages are:

Romans 6:1-4. Here baptism is seen as a symbolic representation of dying, being buried, and rising again with Christ.

1 Corinthians 1:13-17. In this passage Paul does not belittle baptism but protests a misunderstanding at Corinth. In 10:2 he warns against a mechan-

9

ical view of baptism as assuring salvation.

1 Corinthians 12:12, 13. Baptism is the means of incorporation into the Christian community, which is the body of Christ. Through baptism the Spirit is received and the barriers that divided people are overcome.

Galatians 3:26-29. Baptism is a means of "putting on Christ." This union with Christ overcomes all human divisions.

Ephesians 4:5. Baptism and Christian unity are related.

Colossians 2:9-15. Baptism means dying to sin and rising again to a new life through our union with Christ.

An interesting passage is 1 Peter 3:21. "Baptism . . . now saves you . . ." But the context makes it clear that it has that effect only when we are called forth in obedience to a moral and spiritual cleansing and renewed fellowship with God, based on the saving act of Christ.

While our primary focus is on baptism, we should note that other key biblical words, such as *covenant*, are crucial for our understanding of the kingdom of God and the new kingdom community, the church. Baptism may be seen as a rite of response, the covenant of believers to God's covenant with His people. For our understanding of the church and the meaning of church membership, it is also important to remember that the community of God is constituted by a call of God to break with the existing biologically and culturally defined community in order to be planted into a new community. The New Testament church was a missionary church as represented by the Great Commission (Matt. 28:18-20).

Summary   In summary, the biblical passages suggest baptism as:

1. Connected with acceptance of the gospel message
2. An expression of repentance, acceptance of the forgiveness of sins, and the commitment to obedience

10

3. Performed "in the name of Christ" and incorporating people into union with Christ
4. Incorporating the believer into the kingdom community, the church, as the body of Christ, awaiting the Lord's return
5. Incorporating the believer into the community as a worker, carrying on the work of Christ here on earth, calling others to recognize the kingdom and respond in faith

HOW THE CHURCH HAS UNDERSTOOD BAPTISM

From Symbol to Sacrament It is generally agreed that the predominant practice of the early church was believer's baptism. Christian baptism was for those who had received the gospel message, repented of their sins, and desired to follow Christ. The act of baptism was a symbol of this.

As time went on, perhaps under common views of the magical efficacy of external rites, a sacramental value was attached to baptism. Baptism itself came to be seen as effecting forgiveness of sins. Finally, it was seen as indispensable for forgiveness.

Among early Christian writers, Hermas wrote that life is given by the baptismal water, and Barnabas taught that in baptism the Christian enters into possession of salvation. For Irenaeus regeneration and baptism were closely connected. Some see in his writing (about A.D. 180) an allusion to infant baptism, but that is not clear.[2] Tertullian, writing about A.D. 200, urged that children be instructed before baptism, so that they are "led by their own free choice to seek for it with sincere longing of the heart."[3]

In A.D. 253, under Cyprian's influence, sixty-six bishops declared themselves in favor of infant baptism. After Cyprian the baptism of infants became current practice in Africa. With the Constantinian synthesis of the church and society in the fourth century the concept of the mass-church prevailed.

11

Infant baptism came to be seen as the means of accepting the children into Christendom, relieving the descendants of church members of the necessity of making a decision. An obvious result was the "Christianizing" of masses, but the secularizing of the church.

The Protestant Reformation

At the time of the Reformation, the Roman Catholic church taught that baptism was essential to salvation, that it was necessary for the washing away of Original Sin and all sins committed up to baptism, that it conveyed divine grace, and that it should be administered to infants at the earliest possible moment, since they are lost without baptism.

The reformers of the sixteenth century rejected the magical concept of the sacraments. Luther denied that baptism automatically conveyed divine grace, making it conditional upon faith. But by retaining infant baptism he had to speak of a child's "sleeping faith." Zwingli and Calvin (followed by the Reformed churches) held that baptism had no power to convey grace but was only a symbol of acceptance into the church and a pledge to Christian nurture.

These reformers, the Anglicans, and the Roman and Greek Catholics continued to practice infant baptism, however, often requiring it by law in order to maintain a national or mass church.

The Anabaptist Challenge: Believer's Baptism

A more serious challenge to this understanding of the church and baptism was brought by the Anabaptists. On the basis of the New Testament, the Anabaptists understood the church as a people called out by God. Baptism was for believers who through repentance and regeneration of the Spirit chose to follow Christ in life. Searching the Scriptures they discovered no evidence for infant baptism or for the idea that everyone in a particular geographical area is automatically a church member. They came to believe that the church should be made up of those who seek to live a new life of dis-

12

cipleship and who join the fellowship by their own decision, not because the government requires it.

Since the time of the Reformation there have been others besides Mennonites who have emphasized believers' baptism. Among these are the Baptists dating back to the English Separatists of the seventeenth century, and the Church of the Brethren from the early eighteenth century.

Infant Baptism Today

In this century new attention has been focused on the practice of infant baptism, even in state church areas, through the challenge of Karl Barth,[4] and his son, Marcus Barth.[5] In denominations that practice infant baptism new concern is being expressed for liturgical integrity. Baptism is now understood as a "sign" to point people forward to something not yet fully understood or accomplished. Laurence Stookey writes that in baptizing infants or adults, baptism is "the corporate testimony of the community of faith to the action which God brings about in people."[6]

Churches practicing infant baptism today emphasize God's grace to the child. The child is dedicated to the Lord by parents and sponsors. The parents and the church are saying, "We will be faithful in the nurture of this child." Most of the churches that practice infant baptism also have a confirmation service. Confirmation is both a public confession of faith in Jesus Christ as Savior and Lord, and recognition that the person is being received into active membership of the church.

ANABAPTIST-MENNONITE PRACTICE AND UNDERSTANDING

The Schleitheim Confession

The earliest Anabaptist statement of faith, the Schleitheim Confession, begins with this article on baptism:

1. Notice concerning baptism. Baptism shall be given to all those who have been taught repentance and the amendment of life and who believe truly that their sins are taken away through Christ, and to all those

who desire to walk in the resurrection of
Jesus Christ and be buried with Him in death,
so that they might rise with Him; to all
those who with such an understanding themselves desire and request it from us; hereby
is excluded all infant baptism, the greatest
and first abomination of the pope. For
this you have the reasons and the testimony
of the writings and the practice of the
apostles. Matthew 28, Mark 16, Acts 2, 8,
16, 19. We wish simply yet resolutely and
with assurance to hold to the same.[7]

**Grebel,
Blaurock,
and other
Anabaptists**

Rebaptism on the basis of faith was already taking place before Schleitheim. Grebel's letters to
Thomas Müntzer (1524) suggested among other
convictions, the baptism of converted disciples of
Christ.[8] Grebel's break with Zwingli came in the
public debate January 17, 1525, over the question
of baptism. The council mandates that followed,
ordered Grebel and Manz and their associates to
cease their teaching and preaching activity, and
ordered immediate baptism of all unbaptized infants. Thus the stage was set for what happened
that night of January 21, 1525, when the group
met for prayer in a home in Zürich. A priest,
George Blaurock, knelt before Grebel requesting
believer's baptism. Grebel complied, whereupon
others came to him, asking for baptism.

From this meeting the group went out with a
sense of divine mission. Fearing neither Zwingli
nor the council, they went from house to house
and into the towns and villages teaching and preaching and urging men and women everywhere to join
them in their new fellowship. In spite of arrests
and fines and imprisonments, the people responded.
By Easter Balthasar Hubmaier and practically his
whole parish in Waldshut, with 300 adult participants, had been baptized. Grebel had great success
in St. Gallen where about 500 were baptized at one
time.[9]

Because these acts, though based on a rediscovery

of the New Testament, clearly rejected the Church's tradition of infant baptism and undercut the Church-state relationship (as important for Luther and Zwingli as for the Roman church), harrassment, imprisonment, and martyrdom followed. These believers were given the derogatory name "anabaptist" (over-again-baptizers). The death penalty was meted out to these rebaptizers under provisions contained in the Justinian code against heretics. The Anabaptists of the sixteenth century, however, did not consider themselves rebaptizers since they felt infant baptism to be no baptism at all. For them the only true baptism was baptism on confession of faith.

The conversion of Menno Simons, priest in Pingjum, Friesland, was hastened by the incident in the neighboring village of Leeuwarden in 1531 when Sicke Freerks, a tailor, was beheaded for being rebaptized. What stirred Menno was that a pious, God-fearing man should be willing to die for the sake of a second baptism.

Anabaptist Writings About Baptism

As believer's baptism became a visible symbol of their break with the state churches, it is understandable that in defending their views the Anabaptists spoke and wrote much about baptism.

Balthasar Hubmaier distinguished three types of baptism: baptism of the Spirit in regeneration; baptism in water, as the believer pledged his life to God and the church; and baptism in blood, both in a daily death to sin and resurrection to new life, and in the recurrent persecution from the world.[10]

Hubmaier also left an order for the practice of baptism. This called for presentation before the bishop for testing, ability to pray and to explain the articles of Christian faith. Then the candidate was presented to the congregation for prayer and public questions, after which he was baptized. The bishop laid his hands upon the one newly baptized and said:

> I give thee witness and authority, that

15

thou henceforth shalt be numbered among the fellowship of Christians; that as a member of this fellowship thou shalt participate in its keys, and thou shalt break bread and pray with the other Christian sisters and brethren. God be with thee and with thy spirit. Amen.[11]

Hans Hut also wrote of three elements in baptism: the outer covenant which announces the baptized one's faith to the church and enrolls him in its disciplined fellowship; the inner baptism of redemptive suffering through the cross of Christ; and the eschatological sign for the last day. Hut emphasized the covenant aspect in which the church is bound into a disciplined unity.[12]

Melchior Hofmann, whose provocative sermon at Emden in 1530 led to the baptism of 300 believers, soon thereafter published his tract on baptism, *Die Ordonnantie Godts.* This discussion of baptism as commanded in the Great Commission draws on a rich collection of biblical texts and symbols, using the Exodus and wilderness experiences of the Hebrews as a symbol of regeneration in the life of the believer.[13]

Pilgram Marpeck, the most important writer of the German Anabaptists in the sixteenth century, emphasized the unity of the inner and outer baptism. Avoiding the extremes of sacramentalism and spiritualism, he pointed to the active participation in the act of baptism of God, the church, and the one baptized. A key passage for Marpeck was 1 John 5:6-8, about the three witnesses, the Spirit, water, and blood, as pointing to, but also acting in one single baptism.[14]

Menno Simons wrote several tracts on baptism. He refuted the practice of infant baptism on the grounds that Christ commanded His disciples to go out and preach and then baptize the believing. Menno's view was that:

   . . . baptism is a sign of obedience, commanded of Christ, by which we testify when we receive it that we believe the word of the Lord, that we repent of our former life and conduct, that we desire to rise with Christ unto a new life, and that we believe in the forgiveness of sins through Jesus Christ.[15]

Mennonite Practice

With such a strong focus on the issue of baptism during the sixteenth century, most Mennonite groups and congregations have maintained believer's baptism. The minimum requirements for entry into the church has been a personal confession of faith followed by water baptism. In most instances baptism has been seen as a public witness to the experience of salvation, as well as entry into the membership of the congregation.

The usual age of first admission into the church became traditional at fifteen to eighteen in later Mennonite history in Europe and North America. In Holland, emphasis upon a personal, intelligent commitment led to an age for baptism in the early twenties. In Canada, sixteen to nineteen is common, with baptisms also of those of mature years. In the United States thirteen to seventeen is the more usual range. Some congregations baptize young people at age twelve to thirteen, with a few even below age ten.[16] A youth survey taken in the General Conference churches in 1966 revealed that the age of baptism varies from below age thirteen to age twenty-one, with one-fourth baptized below age thirteen.[17] In *Anabaptists Four Centuries Later*, Kauffman and Harder reported that the median age of baptism was 14.0 in the Mennonite Church and 16.4 in the General Conference Mennonite Church (p. 71).

Influences that have lowered the age of baptism in our churches include the Child Evangelism movement, and evangelistic services in which converts are often baptized and received into church membership a few weeks later with a short period of instruction. Other practices include the emphasis on

17

Sunday school and the church camps as a place for making commitments. The use of catechism came into the Mennonite church in the middle of the seventeenth century (in Holland). Today most Mennonite churches in North America carry on some form of catechism or prebaptismal instruction.

The Mode of Baptism The two common forms of baptism are (1) immersion, in which the person enters and is covered by water, or (2) pouring (also sprinkling) in which only a small amount of water is placed on the applicant's head. Pouring is sometimes from a pitcher or by cupped hands taking water from a basin.

Pouring is the form most commonly used in Mennonite churches.[18] Because emphasis has been on inward meanings rather than outward forms, Mennonites have recognized other forms also. The symbol is less important than that which it symbolizes. Thus there are individual congregations who use immersion, and other congregations have honored the request of persons for whom immersion has special meaning. In some of the overseas churches, as in Colombia and Zaire, immersion became the common practice.

What are the reasons for immersion or for pouring? The arguments in favor of immersion include:
1. Early meanings of the word *baptism* include to dip or to immerse.
2. John baptized where there was much water and in the Jordan.
3. The illustration Paul uses in Romans 6 of the believer dying and rising with Christ seems especially appropriate when one thinks of immersion.
4. Early church writings like the *Teaching of the Twelve Apostles* hint at immersion. Many historians think immersion was the usual practice.

Arguments in favor of sprinkling or pouring include:
1. The word *baptism* also has meanings other than to dip or immerse. It is used of washing and cleansing acts.

18

2. To speak of John baptizing *in* the Jordan may mean only geographical location.
3. Romans 6 emphasizes the believer's death to sin and renewal in righteousness rather than a form of baptism.
4. Early church writings also refer to pouring.
5. Pouring is symbolic of the activity of the Holy Spirit coming from above to cleanse, indwell, and empower for discipleship.[19]

We must conclude that both forms were used from earliest times. To argue for the validity of one and deny the validity of the other is to miss the point of baptism. Consequently, though pouring has been the usual mode among our churches, we do not deny the validity of any other mode.[20]

II. SUGGESTIONS FOR OUR PRACTICE OF BAPTISM

After looking at the biblical passages and the history of baptism over nearly twenty centuries, we turn now to the contemporary practice of this ordinance. With such a wide range of meanings and practices, what follows must be seen as suggestions.

CLARIFYING WHAT WE SAY BY BAPTISM

Questions About Baptism — Congregations (and pastors) develop patterns of doing things. Those patterns tend to become fixed. Periodically it is important to stop and ask "Why?" Here are questions that need to be asked about baptism.

How is baptism related to conversion and the experience of salvation? Is baptism the confirmation of faith in Christ? Is a person lost unless he is baptized? How do we understand conversion for people for whom there is not an "about face"?

How is baptism related to church membership and the church's mission? Is baptism the act of incorporating persons into the life of the church? If not baptism, how and when does this happen? Is baptism graduation or commencement (beginning)?

19

Is instruction and growth to come before, or after, or both?

In what ways is baptism a means of grace and so a sacramental act of God? What happens in baptism beyond what we bring to the act?

Meanings of Baptism

Let us look at what we have already said about baptism. In *Off to a Good Start*, baptism is described as "the symbol of being included in the family of God and is administered to those who have received Christ through repentance and personal faith. Baptism is a seal by which the congregation recognizes what the spirit of God has done in your life."[1]

In *This We Believe*, baptism is described as "our conscious, deliberate, public identification with God and His people. . . . In baptism we cast our lot with the *community of the Spirit*, and God's mission for the whole world."[2] Or again the definition of baptism is given as, "The ordinance of the church by which an individual publicly witnesses to his faith in Jesus Christ as his personal Savior and pledges his life to Him in obedience and is received into the fellowship of the church."[3]

Baptism in a Believers' Church

When the believers' church is taken seriously, there is more to joining the church than joining a service club such as Rotary or Lions or 4-H. Martin Luther, though doubting that enough such people could be found, described the believers' church as those who "want to be Christian in earnest and who profess the gospel with hand and mouth," those who "sign their names and meet alone in a house," those who perform Christian works, "those who accept the necessity of being reproved, corrected, cast out, or excommunicated," those who give willingly to the poor, those who develop orderly group practices including baptism, and those who "center everything on the Word, prayer, and love."[4]

Baptism and membership in this kind of church is serious business. The fact that our congregations

20

are imperfect expressions of the believers' church does not mean that we should make church membership cost nothing. When people are asked to commit little, the church means little. Baptism is the beginning of a life of consecrated discipleship. Baptism can be the real beginning of growth in the Christian life and in the mission of the church.

Separating Baptism and Church Membership Some congregations have separated baptism and church membership, especially for younger people. The first act recognizes the person's commitment to Christ. The second, after a period of instruction and training, involves an act of commitment to the church, and acceptance of membership in the congregation. This raises the question of the commitment of children.

It is important to confirm the decision experiences of children and recognize the validity of their commitments. However, it is also important to distinguish between the religion of childhood (a framework of innocence) and a Christian experience which is based on faith and repentance (a framework of responsibility).[5]

We need to recognize in children these motivations: the strong need to belong, the fear of eternity, and the desire to please parents. If salvation simply means accepting Christ as Savior, then a child can of course do this. Salvation is a gift (Eph. 2:8, 9), but it is not cheap (Eph. 4:1; 5:1, 2). If we understand salvation as acceptance also of the lordship of Christ to lead us into a life of discipleship, then a child may not be ready for the commitment implied in baptism. Baptism is for those who are ready to devote themselves to a local community of faith where the life of discipleship and the activities of admonition and encouragement are part of the common life. We should be cautious about using baptism as a device to hold the children while they are young so that they don't get away unbaptized when they are older. That kind of baptism has little meaning and may innoculate them

21

against a more meaningful experience later.

The significance of age twelve to thirteen has often been recognized. Recall Jesus' journey with His parents to the temple (Luke 2:42), or the Jewish ceremony of *bar mitzvah* by which it is affirmed that a boy has reached the age of religious responsibility, normally his thirteenth birthday. One way of recognizing this achievement in our churches might be to celebrate the child's twelfth or thirteenth birthday in a service and appoint an adult to relate to the person over the next several years in a discipling relationship.[6] But baptism would come after the young person has worked through some of the adolescent feelings of rebellion and has made a personal and deliberate choice (when there is also the freedom to say "no") to turn from a self-centered life to follow Christ as Lord as a member of the church.

Another caution for separating baptism and church membership is that people should not see themselves baptized into Christ apart from the Christian community. Beware the individualism of our day that sees decisions and commitments as "private" acts. They are personal, but not private. *People of God* and *community of faith* are concepts that remind us of the corporate aspect of the church, of divine grace, and of Christian commitment! A baptismal service which does not provide a relationship to the visible church does not fully symbolize the meaning of the act.[7]

Baptism as Public Witness

Though baptism is a personal commitment, it is also a public celebration. Though baptism is related to a person's past, and an act of Christ in the past, it is today! Let us value the moment as a witness. In baptism we celebrate not only the person's rebirth in Christ, but also the person's entry into community with us. A new believer is not just the concern of the parents and family, but the concern of us all. The gospel is that we are members of one another, responsible for one another. Church mem-

22

bership is a way of ordering our life in community.

Summary   In summary, the specific age is less important than whether the person is a believer, with freedom to make a choice to follow or reject Christ, and willingness to take responsibility for others in the community of faith. We should, however, not expect decisions of faith below the age of accountability. As a congregation we need to develop our understanding of what we are trying to say by the act of baptism as we practice it.

Has your church council, board of deacons, or elders group recently evaluated your understanding and practice of baptism? A helpful study will involve not only pastor and young people, but parents, congregational leaders, and hopefully the entire congregation. Examine also the ways in which your congregation provides experiences for children and young people that lead to covenant making.[8]

PREPARING FOR BAPTISM AND CHURCH MEMBERSHIP

Instruction for persons baptized and joining the church is essential. A listing of instruction resources may be found in Appendix A, page 51.

Teachers need to be free to adapt materials. But there is need for understanding of adolescent development, of how learning takes place, of education as a process, and of the wide range of teaching resources beyond reading, writing, lecture and discussion (such as films, field trips, personal experiences, drama, people from the congregation, the class members themselves, etc.). Above all, it is important to remember that the person is more important than the curriculum.

Finally, in looking for instruction materials, the pastor should not neglect the Bible as the basic resource book. The prolonged contact with young people provided by the catechism class is one of the best opportunities to introduce persons to the salvation story of the Bible, the major themes of the biblical witness, and guidance in use of the Bible for study and devotional reading.

Youth Class Suggestions

Following are some suggestions for the church membership class for young people:

1. A decision needs to be made about the best time and setting for instruction. In some churches the catechism class meets during the Sunday school hour. In others catechism is conducted after school, Saturday, or Sunday for those who respond to the specific invitation. Recognize what it means when a Sunday school class automatically becomes the catechism class and there are no options *but* to attend. Baptism is the sign of the act of taking up the new life in Christ.

2. The length of a course of study is variable. Twelve weeks would seem minimum. Some churches use two years. Most use at least nine to twelve months if the class is during Sunday school time.

3. The scope of material should include the teachings of the Bible and the Christian faith, opportunity for personal encounter with the Scriptures and application of its meaning for self, the history of the church and of our faith heritage, God's purpose for the church, and the local congregation's practice of faith.

4. The attitude in class may be more important than the materials. Faith assertions are important, but the task of teacher is to facilitate growth in faith and ability to choose wisely, rather than to instill a set of right answers. Thus prebaptism instruction needs to be personal and relational. At least one or two personal visits with each class member by the teacher may be helpful to clarify the person's self-understanding as a Christian and to build a relationship of trust.

5. Who does the teaching? The pastor? Other members of the congregation? Have you con-

24

sidered a team, utilizing the gifts and witness of several congregational leaders? Another possibility is to have each member of the class name a "partner-in-faith" from the congregation and allow a relationship of support to develop. Some congregations plan a parallel "catechism" class for parents as a way of the congregation and home relating at this crucial time for the adolescent.

6. The request for baptism should also be processed by other persons along with the pastor. Does your congregation involve parents? deacons? the congregation? A minimum readiness for baptism might include the person's being able to say with certainty, "I am a follower of Christ and I want my life to count for Christ and for the Church." A helpful "Readiness for Baptism and Church Membership Questionnaire" and paper "Are You Ready for Baptism?" by James Schrag is included as Appendix B. Note that it is written specifically for young people age sixteen or older. Baptism should be timed with the working of the Spirit in people's hearts and their readiness to take up the Christian walk. This is why some congregations have moved to a more individually coached process of preparation for baptism rather than periodic classes.

Planning and Flexibility Congregations will find it helpful to plan specific times to focus on commitment. In spring the church festivals of Easter or Pentecost seem especially appropriate. In the fall, October or November are good months to focus on the life of the church.

In addition to planning systematically, there is need for spontaneity and flexibility. To the question, "What prevents me from being baptized now?" we must at times say, "Nothing." (Acts 8:36-38.) Yet we must be aware that people at a high emotional moment may want to be baptized right now, with no real readiness to make a commitment of responsibility. Then after the event, when the

25

mood has peaked, the experience may seem empty. An authentic experience of faith involves persons also in making realistic commitments.

Instruction for Adults

Following are some suggestions for an inquirer's class for adults:

1. Meeting in homes will help build personal relationships and group experiences.
2. Involve a couple or several members of the congregation to foster assimilation of newcomers.
3. Plan for a maximum of ten to twelve sessions. Perhaps six is adequate.
4. An outline might include:
   Getting acquainted and sharing spiritual pilgrimage
   Salvation in Christ and spiritual growth
   Church history (including Mennonite heritage)
   Teachings of the Christian church (with specific attention to believers' baptism, discipleship, peace witness, etc.)
   The mission of the church (conference/local)
   Two helpful course outlines for adult classes are provided in *Focus on Faith* (see Appendix I, p. 162) by Wilfred Unruh and Leonard Wiebe (p. 203-4).
5. Study Booklets: Burton G. Yost's *Finding Faith and Fellowship* (Newton, Kansas: Faith and Life Press, 1974) is a thirty-two page booklet written on a popular level and especially helpful to people who have not had a Mennonite background.
   John Paul Wenger's *Because God Loves* (Scottdale, Pa.: Herald Press, 1976) has a similar appeal.
   J. C. Wenger has written a series of five booklets published by Herald Press, Scottdale, Pa. (1977) in The Mennonite Faith Series. Titles are *How Mennonites Came to Be*, *What Mennonites Believe*, *The Way to a New Life*, *The Way of Peace*, and *Disciples of Jesus*.

26

PLANNING THE BAPTISM SERVICE

The Ritual   H. S. Bender described the usual Mennonite baptism ritual as follows:

> The candidate is asked a series of questions regarding his basic faith, after which he is asked to pledge renunciation of the world and its sin as well as faithful obedience to Christ and His Word, and submission to the rules and regulations of the church which he is about to join. Thereupon the elder or minister baptizes him (in the mode of pouring or sprinkling the candidate kneels during the ceremony), then welcomes him into the fellowship of the church by the right hand of fellowship and, in some groups by the kiss of brotherhood.[9]

Variations in the ritual are many. That is good. Ritual dare not become mechanical.

Individual or Group?   One of the first questions in planning the baptism service is whether it will be an individual or a group experience. Some congregations have moved to individualizing the experience, baptizing each person when readiness is expressed. The value of this is that the baptism service can be made more intimately their own. Baptism then involves a "stepping forward" on one's own initiative. Persons who are older often like to help plan their baptism service, perhaps choosing hymns or other music, and asking friends to participate.

The value of the group experience in which several persons are baptized in the same service lies in the encouragement of others. Some persons need others to "step forward" with them. Whether baptized alone or along with others, it is important that each one's baptism be personal.

Baptism as Celebrative Service   Celebration is the mood of baptism. We need to take time to celebrate with those who take up the life of the kingdom. Suggestions to magnify this service in the life of the congregation are:

1. Plan baptism when most of the congregation can

27

attend, at the Sunday morning worship service, or in a special Sunday evening service. Baptism can be anyplace—in the sanctuary, outside at a river or lake, in a home. But can the congregation be involved and enter into this experience? In special situations of baptism in the hospital, or of someone who becomes ill in crowds, it is helpful to involve at least one or more others of the church to represent the congregation.

2. Plan for the service in advance. Publish the names of those who will be baptized, inviting counsel, affirmation and prayer on their behalf.

3. Plan a series of services that will involve the congregation. This could include a) presentation of the candidates in which they share their statements of faith with the congregation and in which others of the congregation give witness and encouragement; b) a service which focuses on the meaning of faith, the vows made in baptism, the responsibilities of church membership; and c) the service of baptism in which there is renunciation of evil, celebration of God's redeeming love, and a vow to follow Christ. Sometimes these elements are combined in one service. (See a suggested order on page 30.)

4. Be aware of rich meanings the symbols of baptism can bring to the service:
   a) Stepping forward - a crossing over (exodus) into the community that already is taking up the life of the age to come
   b) Speaking - witness as a follower of Jesus
   c) Kneeling - submission to Christ as Lord, and to each other
   d) Water - a repentant spirit, cleansing by Christ as Savior
   e) Pouring water - receiving into one's life the power and presence of the Holy Spirit
   f) Laying on of hands - confirming faith, ordaining into the mission of the church
   g) Right hand of fellowship - acceptance and

love and the bond of fellowship in the church.

5. Communion and foot washing can also be part of the baptism service, celebrating our new life in Christ and with each other in the church. As persons are baptized it seems particularly appropriate that they now share in this fellowship of bread and cup, basin and towel.

The Involvement of Congregation and Family

It is important that the congregation share in the service. This can be done by:

1. Singing and prayers
2. A sharing period for words of witness and encouragement
3. Inviting the participation of others in the laying on of hands
4. A reading of a response such as number 725 in *The Mennonite Hymnal* or a liturgy of baptism as on page 34, or repeating together the covenant of membership of the congregation.
5. Greeting those newly baptized following the service. This is often an overwhelming experience for new members—that people care that much!

Acknowledge this special event with a certificate of baptism. The congregation may also wish to give a Bible or appropriate devotional book or other gift as a remembrance of the day of baptism. Some churches post pictures of new members on the bulletin board or use the occasion to introduce new members through their newsletter.

Finally, let us recognize that baptism can be a special family occasion. Though we are called into a "new family" in baptism, this often becomes a time to revitalize faith in the home.

1. Send a letter to the parents, sharing what has been happening in the class and in the life of their son or daughter, inviting them to the baptism service.
2. This is a good occasion for a pastoral visit to the home.
3. Parents can be invited to stand with their children or participate in laying on of hands.

29

4. A personal contact with each parent after the baptism service is appropriate. Often they have feelings they want to express.

BAPTISM SERVICE FORMS

The Order of Service An order for the service might include the following elements:
1. Appropriate opening worship
2. Introduction (including Scripture)
3. Testimony of the candidate(s) for baptism (and witness of others if desired)
4. Vows (questions)
5. The act of baptism
6. The right hand of fellowship
7. The commitment (response) of the congregation
8. Prayer (prayer might also precede act of baptism)

Scriptures

Matthew 3:13-17	1 Corinthians 12:12-13
28:19-20	Galatians 3:26-28
Mark 1:9-11	Ephesians 4:1-7, 11-16
Luke 3:18-22	Philippians 1:3-11
9:57-62	3:7-14
John 1:32-34	Colossians 2:9-15
3:1-21	1 Thessalonians 5:23-24
Acts 2:37-47	2 Timothy 1:3-14
Romans 6:1-11	1 John 5:1-12

Hymns The numbers are as listed in *The Mennonite Hymnal.*

  1 Holy God, We Praise Thy Name
 40 I Sing with Exultation
 43 Immortal, Invisible God
 75 Love Divine, All Loves Excelling
 90 In Thee is Gladness
208 O Holy Spirit, Enter In
228 I Sought the Lord
248 I Lay My Sins on Jesus
265 My Jesus, I Love Thee
291 All My Hope on God Is Founded
300 Be Thou My Vision
353 I Bind My Heart This Tide
354 Just as I Am, Thine Own to Be

30

358 Take My Life and Let it Be Consecrated
376 Glorious Things of Thee Are Spoken
385 Blest Be the Tie That Binds
386 Heart with Loving Heart United
398 O Happy Day, that Fixed My Choice
399 My God, Accept My Heart
539 More Love to Thee, O Christ
544 Blessed Assurance
562 Christ Has for Sin Atonement Made
581 I am Thine, O Lord
606 Praise God From Whom

Introduction to Baptism

"And Jesus came and said to them, 'All authority in heaven and on earth has been given to me. Go therefore and make disciples of all nations, baptizing them in the name of the Father and of the Son and of the Holy Spirit, teaching them to observe all that I have commanded you; and lo, I am with you always, to the close of the age.'" Matthew 28:18-20.

Jesus gave us a commandment and a promise. Because of them we are here today. Because of them people are here to make the covenant of baptism with God and His people. We are witnesses of their choice, but more than that, we are their companions in it.

Baptism is an act both of God and of us. In it God gives us the covenant of a good conscience, as Peter says. It enacts what God has done with us: made us dead unto sin and alive unto himself. In it we also respond to God, letting go of ourselves, dying to ourselves, to be given new life by God's Spirit. It is a public witness of what has happened to us.

Baptism is an act both of a person and a community. It seals our decision to turn from living for ourselves and against God and other people to living for them. John uses the most personal words possible to describe becoming a Christian: it is to be born again, into a new humanity. This new humanity of which we are a part affirms that God is

31

at work, that conversion and baptism are not only the private experience of one person, but acts of God which the church accepts and stands by. Baptism is communal because when we are born again our new life is with others, not against them, most particularly is it with the body of Christ.[10]

Vows (questions)

Here are several alternate forms of vows from which to choose, or adapt in your own words.[11]

Form A

1. Do you now confess faith in Jesus Christ as your Savior from the power and guilt of sin, trusting in the forgiveness and renewing power of God declared through Jesus' death and resurrection?

2. In response to that love, do you now commit yourself to Christ and to His service through the church, and will you seek by the guidance of the Holy Spirit to turn from sin, will you foster communion with God in prayer and the use of His Word, and as far as you know how, lead an upright Christian life?

Form B

1. Do you accept and confess the Lord Jesus Christ as your personal Savior and Redeemer, trusting in His death and resurrection for the forgiveness of your sins?

2. Do you solemnly consecrate yourself to Christ and His service and do you seek by the guidance and power of the Holy Spirit to turn from the ways of sin, foster communion with God in prayer and the use of His Word, and as far as you know how, lead an upright Christian life according to God's revealed will and to the honor of His name?

3. Baptism is also an act of identifying with God's mission for the world. So I ask you now, do you desire to be baptized upon this faith in Christ, and to be received into the church of Jesus Christ, identifying yourself with God's mission for the world through the church?

Form C

1. Are you sorry for your sins, have you turned your life from evil and have you forsaken all other lords for the God and Father of our Lord

32

Jesus Christ, without whom nothing is?

2. Do you believe that Jesus Christ is the Savior of the world and its Lord; that He is your Savior and Lord?

3. Do you want to walk in the resurrection of Christ, made strong and wise by His Spirit, living in the power of His victory of sharing and suffering, forgiving and loving until you die?

4. Do you promise to live your life in His body, giving and receiving counsel, knowing no higher loyalty for your life?

Form D   Do you believe in Christ as your Savior and Lord, and do you now want to commit yourself to Christ's Church?

Form E   You may wish to write your own questions. If faith is seen as an act and life rather than intellectual assent, it is appropriate to begin with questions such as: "Has God given you new life? Has Christ called you into His community? Are you taking up the life of the kingdom of God? How is the Holy Spirit strengthening and guiding your life?"

Statement of Baptism

Form A   (candidate kneeling)
"_____(name) Upon your profession of faith, I baptize you in the name of the Father, of the Son, and of the Holy Spirit. (baptism) Amen."

Form B   "_____(name) Upon your profession of faith in the Lord Jesus Christ as your personal Savior from sin, and your vow of consecration to Him and His service, I baptize you in the name of the Father, and of the Son, and of the Holy Spirit. May the Lord baptize you with the Spirit from above."

Right Hand of Fellowship

Form A   In the name of Christ and the church I now extend to you the right hand of fellowship and welcome you, _____(name), as a (brother, sister) into the church of Christ.

Form B   "Arise, shine for your light has come and the glory

33

of the Lord is upon you." Stand up in the name of Jesus Christ and stand faithful in the faith He has given you. I give you the hand of fellowship and welcome you, _____ (name), into the church of Jesus Christ and into our household of faith (kiss). The peace of Christ be with you.

The Commitment of the Congregation

Form A

You have expressed faith in Jesus by your confession of faith and baptism. We too want to join with you now to share our faith and encouragement. We are glad with you. We rejoice that you have chosen to cast your lot with the community of the Spirit. We want you to grow in faith and in this new relationship with God and with others. And our prayer for you we make also for ourselves, that each of us, and all of us together, may be faithful in the purpose of God's kingdom.

Form B

As we now receive you into the fellowship of the church, we make a covenant with you as we renew our own covenant with our Lord: to bear one another's burdens, to share in the experience of forgiveness, to share in the abundance of this world's goods, to assist each other in times of need, to share our joys and our sorrows, and in all things to work for the common good, thus manifesting God's presence among us to His glory. As we unite with each other now, may we all be joined with Christ our Lord.[12]

A Liturgy of Baptism

The following litany was developed by Harold Bauman for use in the Assembly congregation, Goshen, Indiana:

Congregation:

We have pledged to renounce our sin of self-centered living and to bind ourselves under the authority of Jesus Christ to live in God's holy community, the Church, according to Christ's rule and kingdom.

Minister to applicant(s):

Do you join with these believers gathered to witness your baptism into Christ's body in pledging to

34

	renounce your sin of self-centered living and to bind yourself under the authority of Jesus Christ to live in God's holy community, the Church, according to Christ's rule and kingdom?
Applicant(s):	I do.
Congregation:	We affirm that the God of Abraham, Isaac, Jacob, Miriam, Hannah, and Mary is our God.

We affirm that God has come to us in our likeness taking the form of a servant in Jesus of Nazareth.

That God in Christ suffered the bitterness of our rejection and the stigma of our sin in order to reconcile us into the kingdom, and

That God demonstrated power over sin and death by raising Jesus from the dead and declaring the risen Christ is Lord.

We confess that God has given us new life and freedom in the fullness of the Holy Spirit who is the guide and dynamic of Christ's new community.

We believe that in the end God's kingdom of peace and justice will be fully established and that Jesus Christ will be recognized "Lord of Lords and King of Kings."

We are committed to live our lives in this hope.

Minister to applicant(s):	Do you confess this to be your faith, and do you pledge loyalty to Jesus Christ to live your life in this faith and hope with the power of the Holy Spirit?
Applicant(s):	I do.
Minister:	We baptize you as a witness to God's gracious pledge to forgive and accept you into the people of God through Jesus Christ, as a witness to your pledge of allegiance to Jesus Christ as Lord of your life, and as a witness to God's gracious gift of the Holy Spirit poured out upon you and within you to give you power and to release spiritual gifts through you to the believing community as the Spirit chooses.
Prayers	A. Lord, we offer praise to you, for the fellowship

35

in which we partake. For the church, and these relationships of love and concern and support and a common mission, we speak our thanks, and for these who now come to us with their commitment of faith. Be with _____, _____ , and _____, and with their families. Let your peace be upon them, and us, in Christ's name. Amen.

B. O God, Lord of Life, we praise You that Your Spirit touches our life, and that Your presence surrounds us even now. We speak the words, we do the actions. But only You can know the heart, or cleanse the soul, or accept our commitment. Grant now that this act of baptism may have special meaning for _____ (name), and all of us here. Grant (him/her/ them) joy in these new relationships, sustain (him/her) as Your child, and grant Your grace in (his/her) life. We thank You now also for the church, our Father, and for these times of sharing faith and trust with each other. In Jesus name. Amen.

C. Almighty God, You bring together in communion and fellowship those in every place who call upon the name of our Lord Jesus Christ. We heartily thank You that by the guidance of Your Holy Spirit, these persons have been led to dedicate their lives to You. We pray, Father, that through Your grace, both they and we, may ever continue in this holy fellowship, and believe and live so that we may be found worthy to be numbered among Your saints, through Jesus Christ our Lord. Amen.

AFTER BAPTISM

Often it is easier to draw people into making a commitment than to provide the follow-up experiences that will keep that commitment vital. Here are several suggestions for keeping the baptism event alive.

36

Personal Follow-up   If several have been baptized at a service, bring them together within two weeks of the event to talk about their feelings. Or if it is the baptism of one person, plan a visit within two or three weeks to talk about the experience.

Personally invite those baptized to the next communion service. Relate communion to baptism. As baptism can be the act which once-for-all incorporates us into Christ, so the Lord's Supper is a continuing communion within that fellowship.

Invite persons baptized to witness the next baptism service. They can encourage new persons being baptized. The event will also help them relive and renew again their own high moment of public commitment to Christ.

Face-to-face Groups   If persons baptized are part of a smaller face-to-face group in the congregation it is helpful to have the group celebrate the event with the person. Church consultant Lyle Schaller points out that new adult members who do not become part of a group, accept a leadership role, or become involved in a task during their first year tend to become inactive.[13] The same is true for young people who may not feel part of the body of Christ as represented in the worshiping congregation. And as young people leave home for work, school, service, the need to maintain meaningful personal ties is even more crucial.

The idea of a "partner-in-faith" can be helpful. If a person being baptized has named someone as a "partner-in-faith," that relationship of a mature member of the church praying for, encouraging, caring for, and relating to a new member can strengthen bonds of faith.[14] Having support groups for each person baptized simply enlarges the "partner" idea.

Continuing Instruction   For persons baptized at a young age, continuing instruction in Christian faith is essential. Learning what is expected of a church member and taking one's place in the organizational and service life of

37

the congregation is only part of it. Often the crucial issues are in applying Christian faith to the many life questions such as relationships with parents and peers, how one gets along in school, decisions about life vocation, marriage, etc. Postbaptismal instruction may not depend so much on a course of study as on good interpersonal relationships.

III. RELATED SERVICES

RECEPTION OF MEMBERS BY LETTER AND AFFIRMATION OF FAITH

The Challenge of New People Coming

Most Mennonite congregations accept members by baptism, by transfer of letter, or by affirmation (confession) of faith. If a congregation has a vital life of worship, fellowship, nurture and outreach, people will be drawn to the body life. As congregations we need to be open to new persons and actively invite others to join us, but also allow people to make that choice when they are ready.

Periodic invitations to membership are important. These can come through the pastor, other members, letter, or bulletin announcement. In cultivating the commitment of others, allow their assimilation into the fellowship of the church and its groups. Do not force a commitment, but recognize that there is freedom in commitment, and that we need to help people experience it.

In areas of high mobility (such as a college or university setting) many persons, particularly young adults, do not have the time to work through their feelings about church membership. Some congregations choose to consider the local active participants as being the "congregation," with minimal concern for the more formalized membership. It is important that friends of the church be given every opportunity to belong. At

38

the same time if membership in the church is to have meaning, a commitment of gifts (time, energy, money, self) seems essential.

When a person is ready to unite with the congregation the following steps may be taken:

Procedures for Receiving Members

1. Arrange for the transfer of church letter from the former congregation. There is value for the persons themselves taking the initiative in requesting the letter. After reception of the person acknowledgement should be sent to the former church.
2. For persons previously baptized, but for whom there is no letter available, a clear affirmation of faith can be a means of identifying with the congregation.
3. Names of persons desiring to unite with the congregation should be shared with the proper leadership body of the congregation. New members should be related to the church through more persons than the pastor.
4. A personal statement in the presence of the congregation (why I want to belong to the church, my faith pilgrimage, my hope for the church, and my commitment to it) will help persons think through the meaning of this new relationship. It will also introduce them to the congregation.
5. Persons, transferring by letter or coming by affirmation, who were baptized as infants or children in another Christian tradition should be invited to baptism on the basis of their present faith. In practice, some congregations acknowledge the validity of baptism and confirmation in another tradition, and accept the affirmation of faith now as more important than baptism as a ritual act. It is important that we do not present the issue of baptism as a barrier to persons. Rather, let us help persons seeking meaningful membership discover the joy and freedom of the meanings to which baptism witnesses.

A Service of Reception

Following is a simple service for receiving new members:

1. Introduce candidate and invite (his/her) faith statement.
2. Question: "Do you desire to be received as a member into this congregation, and are you willing, with the Lord's help, to share the gifts God gives you with us, in our common mission as servants of Jesus Christ?"
3. Right hand of fellowship: "On behalf of the congregation I now extend to you the right hand of fellowship and welcome you, _____(name), as a (brother, sister) into the membership of this congregation.
4. The congregation's commitment. (Form B on page 34 is appropriate.)

Associate Membership

In areas of high mobility, such as a college setting or for young people in short-term service, there is often a desire to feel a closer bond with a congregation, but yet not readiness to sever the relationship to the home church. Then associate membership can be appropriate.

One congregation in such a setting declares:

Persons accepting the statement of faith and practice, who are members in good standing of other congregations, and who desire to be temporarily associated with the congregation, shall be received as associate members. Associate members are granted the rights of full membership, except for holding elective office, and are expected to accept the duties of membership as long as their association with the congregation is active.[1]

It should be understood that associate membership is for a temporary period. It terminates when persons leave. After two or three years, full membership should be the relationship. Nonresident membership over several years (even for students) has little meaning. People should be encouraged to become members of an actual congregation of the body of Christ wherever they live and work.

When members move away we need to encourage them to identify with a congregation near their new home.

1. Discuss the value of a church relationship where they live before they move.
2. Share with them information regarding the names and addresses of the nearest Mennonite churches in the area, and also inform the pastor of a person or family moving into their area.
3. Write periodic (at least twice a year) letters to nonresident members, telling about congregational events. Also invite them to share information about their work, life, and church relationship. When people who have moved do not transfer their membership, it is appropriate to find out what is wrong.
4. When members request a letter of transfer, send it promptly, rejoicing with them in their new relationship.

COVENANT RENEWAL

In every congregation there are those for whom membership in the church loses its meaning. Sometimes people have not really committed themselves. Sometimes they have been hurt by other members of the church. Sometimes the church has failed to exercise its role of "binding and loosing" (Matt. 16:18; 18:15-22), of confronting and encouraging in love.

Membership termination must be practiced by the congregation with extreme care and love. The congregation must work gently and patiently with those who withdraw themselves from fellowship. But to neglect fellow members and withhold discipline or love hurts both the congregation and the member.

However, the relationship to the church sometimes does become meaningless to persons. People become inactive members and withdraw their pres-

41

ence, if not their name from the membership list. If we have made sensitive and prayerful efforts to hear their hurts, needs, concerns, we need also to respect their choice to withdraw from fellowship.

Opportunities to Renew Commitment

For those whose life with the congregation continues year after year, there should be times to renew the covenant. Here are possibilities:

1. In October a letter might be sent to nonresident members both for the purpose of maintaining contact, and inviting recommitment in the coming year. Nonresident members might be asked to respond with either a) some indication of continuing commitment, b) a request for transfer of letter to another church, or c) a request for withdrawal of their name from the membership roll.

2. Local inactive members might be sent a similar letter (though personal contact is far better in that it gives opportunity to hear hurts and concerns).

3. An annual covenant-renewal service might be held the first Sunday of January. When people become members they are invited to sign a commitment form. At the beginning of each year there is opportunity to renew this commitment. One congregation using an annual renewal-covenant describes their process: Each member who signed is counseled regarding stewardship in commitment in five areas:

   a) Stewardship of attendance (How much of the regular schedule of the church can you commit yourself to?)

   b) Stewardship of gifts and talents (Will you give of yourself to share your talents and spiritual ministries among us?)

   c) Stewardship of counsel (Will you commit yourself to seek counsel from the church and will you give of the discernment the Lord may give you to be ministered within the body?)

   d) Stewardship of prayer (Will you commit yourself to a regular time of prayer for the leadership of the congregation?)

e) Stewardship of finances (Will you commit a regular portion of your income to the local fellowship?)[2]

Other congregations may choose a less rigorous approach. Other ideas are:

a) A Love Feast-Communion Service on the first Sunday of the year with emphasis on sharing, including the sharing of commitments. The Love Feast as practiced by the Church of the Brethren and some Mennonite congregations is a simple meal served at tables. It includes singing, sharing of faith experiences, and then the service of communion at the tables.

b) An every member visit at the beginning of the year. It is better if this visit is not primarily to solicit budget support. The visit should include the invitation to commitment of money, but needs to be a time to interpret the congregation's mission and to hear the needs and concerns of members.

c) An offering of gifts (talent, leadership, ideas, money) in November.

Covenant-Renewal Resources
A few "covenant" Scripture passages are Exodus 19:1-6; Deuteronomy 26:5-11; Joshua 24:1-28; Matthew 26:26-29; 1 Peter 2:4-10.

The following commitment can be used to focus renewal of covenant:

Acknowledging that the church is the Body of Christ, and that the congregation is an expression of the church in the world, I want to commit myself again to Christ and help make this congregation

1. A community of sharing (Acts 2:42, 46)

_____ by regular attendance at the services of worship

_____ by participating in at least one smaller fellowship group as _____

_____ by acts of mutual helpfulness as _____

_____

_____ by giving regularly a portion of my money to the work of the church

43

2. A community of forgiveness (Matt. 16:18, 19; 18:15-20)

    ___ by examining strained relationships between myself and a brother or sister in the congregation, and seeking restoration by asking forgiveness or expressing forgiveness

    ___ by giving and receiving counsel and admonition

3. A community of gifts (Rom. 12, 1 Cor. 12, Eph. 4)

    ___ by offering again my gifts within the church

    ___ by assessing what gifts I can share with the larger community

    ___ by affirming the gift(s) of someone each week

4. A community of peace (Eph. 2:11-22)

    ___ by working toward the good welfare and health (wholeness) of the persons with whom I share home, neighborhood, work

    ___ by recommitting myself to help the church become a more effective instrument for world peace through the following action

_____

5. A missionary community (Matt. 28:18-20)

    ___ by helping to build up this fellowship

    ___ by sharing in some way the reality of God's love with a neighbor, schoolmate, or fellow worker

    ___ by supporting the church's world-wide mission with contributions of money and prayers.

        Name _____

        Date _____

The following covenant can be used as a unison commitment:

    We commit ourselves to follow Jesus Christ, through whom God has made friends with the world and in whom we continue the work of reconciliation.

We commit ourselves to each other, the church, to love our brothers and sisters in God's family, sharing our time, our decisions, our love, talents, and our possessions for everyone's good.

We commit ourselves to care for the world, to bring good news to the poor, and set free the oppressed, to proclaim Jesus as the liberator and Lord.

We commit ourselves to the way of the cross, to a life of simplicity and prayer; in this we will find our joy, our peace and a new life.[3]

PARENT-CHILD DEDICATION

The Purpose   In a parent-child dedication the focus is on the responsibility of the parents and the congregation. The child is recognized as God's gift with the potential to be God's blessing to others. In bringing the child forward, parents are saying, "We want to be faithful to this child. We want to make our home a place where this child may learn to know God, to experience love, and to learn service to others."

As the congregation witnesses this act, we are saying, "We want to support you as parents, in the nurture and encouragement of these children, so that they may learn to know Christ as their Savior and Lord, and choose to become part of the Christian way through the church."

A Sample   1. Appropriate Scriptures include: 1 Samuel 1:21-
Service   28; Matthew 18:10; Mark 9:36, 37; Mark 10:13-16; Luke 2:21, 22, 52.

2. Hymns from *The Mennonite Hymnal*:
   335 Children of the Heavenly Father
   413 Shepherd of Tender Youth
   414 Jesus, Friend, So Kind
   415 O Jesus Christ, Our Lord Most Dear[4]

3. Ask the parents to bring the child forward and ask the question:
   a) "Do you now bring this child in this act of dedication in the desire that (he/she) may grow

45

in the knowledge and love of God? And do you rededicate your home as a place where the spiritual nature of your child may unfold and grow; and by teaching and example so try to lead your child that (he/she) may be able to respond in faith in the love of God through Jesus Christ our Lord?" (The response may be "I do'" or "we do.")

b) "Do you now accept the trust that God places in you for the care and nurture of this child, and do you desire with the help of God and the church to be faithful to this child as Christian parents?" (The response may be "I do," or "we do.")

4. A spoken blessing may include these words:
a) "_____(name of child), I dedicate you to the Christian faith and to the service of others, in the name of the Father, and the Son, and the Holy Spirit. Amen."

b) "_____(name of child), may the love of God, and the gracious spirit of Christ, and the fellowship of God's people bless your life."

5. The congregation's commitment (unison):
a) "You have offered your child to the strong and tender providence of God, and to the nurture of the church. We accept with humility of spirit and seriousness of purpose our responsibility for the spiritual well-being of this child. By our example and our words we will support your parental role. We pray that the life and witness of each of us will make your task both joyful and fruitful."[5]

b) "As your friends and fellow believers we thank God for the gift of your child. By word and by example we will support your parental role of providing a loving home where trust in God may grow. We pray that our life and witness will make your task joyful and fruitful."

6. A brief prayer may follow. It is appropriate to

46

give the parents a certificate of dedication for
their child.
7. An alternate suggestion is to have a children's
choir sing. A good selection of children's hymns
may be found in *The Children's Hymnary* (Faith
and Life Press, 1968) and *Our Hymns of Praise*
(Herald Press, 1958).

FOOTNOTES

I. THE BASIS FOR BAPTISM

1. Henry Poettcker, *A Study on Baptism* (Newton, Kansas: Faith and Life Press, 1963) p. 6.
2. Paul K. Jewett, *Infant Baptism and the Covenant of Grace* (Grand Rapids: William B. Eerdmans, 1978), pp. 25-27.
3. H. S. Bender, "Infant Baptism," *Mennonite Encyclopedia* (Scottdale, Pa.: Mennonite Publishing House, 1955), III, pp. 37-8. This work will hereafter be cited as *ME*.
4. Karl Barth, *Die Kirchliche Lehre von der Taufe* (Zürich, 1943). Translated, *The Teaching of the Church Concerning Baptism.*
5. Marcus Barth, *Die Taufe-ein Sakrament?* (Evangelischer Verlag A. Zollikon-Zurich, 1951).
6. Laurence Stookey, "Baptism and Liturgical Integrity Reconsidered," *The Christian Century*, LXXXVI:35 (August 27, 1969), p. 1111.
7. Michael Sattler, "The Schleitheim Confession" (1527), in John H. Yoder, (trans. and ed.) *The Legacy of Michael Sattler* (Scottdale, Pa.: Herald Press, 1973), p. 36.
8. John C. Wenger, (trans.) *Conrad Grebel's Programmatic Letters of 1524* (Scottdale, Pa.: Herald Press, 1970).

9. H. S. Bender, *Conrad Grebel* (Goshen, Ind.: Mennonite Historical Society, 1950), p. 143.
10. Rollin S. Armour, *Anabaptist Baptism* (Scottdale, Pa.: Herald Press, 1966), p. 92.
11. *Ibid.*, pp. 143-4.
12. *Ibid.*, pp. 76, 95.
13. *Ibid.*, pp. 100-101.
14. *Ibid.*, p. 127.
15. J. C. Wenger (ed.) *The Complete Writings of Menno Simons* (Scottdale, Pa.: Herald Press, 1956) p. 125.
16. H. S. Bender, "Admission into the Church," *ME*, I, p. 13.
17. *Educational News Bulletin* by the Board of Education and Publication, General Conference Mennonite Church, Newton, Kansas, Summer, 1966, pp. 7-8.
18. In the Mennonite Brethren Church immersion is used.
19. Poettcker, *op. cit.*, pp. 12-25. See also James H. Waltner, *This We Believe* (Newton, Kansas: Faith and Life Press, 1968), pp. 142-3.
20. "Our Mode of Baptism," pamphlet prepared by the Committee of the Ministry of the General Conference (Newton, Kansas, 1956).

II. SUGGESTIONS FOR OUR PRACTICE OF BAPTISM
1. Ernest D. Martin (Scottdale, Pa.: Mennonite Publishing House, 1971), p. 27.
2. Waltner, *op. cit.*, p. 144.
3. *Ibid.*, p. 145
4. Martin Luther, quoted by C. J. Dyck in a paper "Membership in the Believers' Church," published in Larry Kehler (ed.) *Focus on Faith* (Newton, Kansas: Faith and Life Press, 1978), p. 3.
5. Evelyn Miller, "When Your Child Wants to Join Church at an Early Age," *Christian Living*, XXV:10 (October, 1978), p. 34.

6. Kehler, *op. cit.*, pp. 148-9.
7. *Affirming Our Faith in Word and Deed* (Scottdale, Pa.: Mennonite Publishing House, 1978) p. 43.
8. John H. Westerhoff III, *Will Our Children Have Faith?* (New York: The Seabury Press, 1976) challenges many of our assumptions regarding the Christian education process. The book examines ways in which we can help persons to an "owned faith."
9. H. S. Bender, "Baptism," *ME*, I, p. 227.
10. Adapted from a baptism service planned by John Rempel, chaplain, Conrad Grebel College.
11. Note that additional baptism forms may also be found in the *Ministers Manual* (Newton, Kansas: General Conference Board of Publication, 1950), pp. 43ff., and *Mennonite Church Polity* Scottdale, Pa.: Mennonite Publishing House, 1944), pp. 101ff.
12. *The Mennonite Hymnal*, No. 725.
13. Lyle Schaller, *Assimilating New Members* (Nashville: Abingdon, 1978), p. 77.
14. Ernest D. Martin, *Preparing for Church Membership* (Scottdale, Pa.: Mennonite Publishing House, 1971), pp. 103-4 outlines suggestions for "Sponsors for New Members."

III. RELATED SERVICES

1. From the constitution (1977) of the Mennonite Church of Normal, Normal, Illinois, p. 5.
2. Mimeographed paper by Walter J. Fahrer, pastor, Northridge Christian Fellowship, Springfield, Ohio.
3. From the December 31, 1978, bulletin of the Grace Mennonite Church, St. Catharines, Ontario.
4. Note also "Friend of the Home," number 550 in *The Brethren Hymnal* (Elgin, Illinois: House of the Church of the Brethren, 1951).
5. Adapted from *The Mennonite Hymnal*, No. 729.

APPENDIX A

RESOURCES FOR INSTRUCTION

1. *Because God Loves*, by John Paul Wenger (Herald Press, 1976).
   Written as a devotional statement of faith to instruct new believers at Grace Chapel in Saginaw, Michigan, the book contains a covenant and twenty-one short meditations. This book will be of special interest to young churches wishing to incorporate adults, young and old, into their fellowship.

2. *Beginning the Christian Life*, by Russell Krabill (Herald Press, 1958).
   This study book, consisting of twelve lessons is used by some congregations to instruct persons in the upper elementary grades for church membership; it can also be used for older youth. A teacher's manual is available.

3. *Focus on Faith* (Faith and Life Press, 1978).
   Compiled and edited by Larry Kehler, this looseleaf manual brings together materials and descriptions of catechism classes of twelve General Conference pastors. Included are several helpful articles and a resource guide, "Pilgrimage of Faith" from the Mennonite Publishing House.

4. *Guide to Faith*, by Helmut Harder (Faith and Life Press, 1979).

This handbook for church membership was written for grades 11 and 12 and other adults. It deals with seventeen important theological concepts of the Christian faith, and relates them to the Anabaptist-Mennonite point of view.

5. *Preparation for the Covenant Life*, by Frank Keller (Faith and Life Press, 1979).
This is a pupil book for young people at the grade 10 and 11 level. Its focus is on the Bible as the salvation story of God's people and on the Christian life as a covenant relationship with God and the church.

6. *Preparing for Church Membership* (Mennonite Publishing House, 1971).
This study course was designed to help congregations do a better job of nurturing new believers and to lead believers into meaningful church membership. It includes a devotional guide (*Off to a Good Start*), a leader's guide (*Preparing for Church Membership*), a historical, doctrinal, and practical resource book for students (*Experiencing Christ in the Church*), and a study of the Sermon on the Mount (*The Christian Way*).
These materials are planned for use in the context of a group conversational experience.

7. *This We Believe*, by James H. Waltner (Faith and Life Press, 1968).
Its twenty-eight chapters contain a systematic presentation of the basic doctrines of the Christian faith. A leader's guide is available.

8. *We Believe*, by Paul Erb (Herald Press, 1969).
This book, a commentary on the twenty articles of the Mennonite Confession of Faith, adopted by the Mennonite General Conference in 1963. Each lesson contains an article of faith, commentary on that article, discussion questions, and suggestions for additional activity. *We Believe* is a self-contained study guide requiring no leader's manual.

APPENDIX B

This questionnaire and paper on "Readiness for Baptism" was prepared by James Schrag, Newton, Kansas.

READINESS FOR BAPTISM AND CHURCH MEMBERSHIP QUESTIONNAIRE

Name _____ Date _____ Age___

Please answer all of the following questions honestly saying how you feel at this time. Your answers will be held in confidence and will not be shared with anyone else without your permission.

Complete the following sentences with the words that first pop into your mind.

1. (choose a, b, or c)
   a) I am a Christian because _____
   _____
   b) I am not a Christian because _____
   _____
   c) I don't know whether I am a Christian because _____
2. My relationship with God is _____
3. Jesus Christ means most to me when_____
   _____
4. Sometimes I wish I were_____

53

5. For me, this school year is going _____
   _____

6. My relationship with my parents is _____
   _____

7. My friends mean most to me when_____
   _____

8. Thinking about next year, I feel_____
   _____

9. I will be ready for baptism when I _____
   _____

10. My feelings about baptism and church membership as they apply to me now are _____
    _____

11. The thing that scares me most about baptism and church membership is _____
    _____

12. The greatest benefit of baptism and church membership is _____

13. The greatest disadvantage of baptism and church membership is _____

14. I am feeling unfair pressure for me to be baptized coming from _____

15. Knowing Jesus taught that we are to be baptized, I feel_____

I think I will be ready for baptism and church membership
    _____ at the end of this class (this summer)
    _____ within six months
    _____ within a year
    _____ after more than a year
I prefer to be baptized
    _____ by myself
    _____ with one or two others
    _____ with my whole class

If you say you are not ready for baptism and church membership now (within the next 2-3 months), what do you have to do or have to become ready? Check all of the following that apply to your life now.

_____ I need to become more mature.

_____ I need to get along better with my parents.

_____ I need to "settle down."

_____ I need to solve my problems with my boy/girl friend.

_____ I need more (or better) friends.

_____ I need to get along better with my teachers.

_____ I need to feel like I am "worth something."

_____ I need to get a better hold on my future.

_____ I need to live a better Christian life.

_____ I need to find someone who will listen to me and understand me.

_____ I am not a Christian and would need to become one.

_____ I need to feel like others in the church want me.

_____ I need to be rid of certain kinds of sin in my life.

_____ I need to know more about what the Mennonite church believes.

_____ I need to know more about what the Bible teaches.

_____ I need help in my prayer life.

_____ I need to know that I am accepted by others.

_____ I need to be better able to assume some of the duties of membership.

The things listed above represent a variety of concerns in your life some of which you may feel quite strongly about. Problems or uncertainty in even a few of these areas can make you feel "not ready" for baptism. It is important for you to realize that no Christian can say that they "have arrived" at final solutions to many of these concerns. At different times in your life some of these concerns will seem more important than others.

Being ready for baptism does not mean that you have to have definite answers for all of these concerns. We are always in a process of growing. It may be important, however, to use this list as a "checkup" on your Christian growth and to speak to the pastor or another trusted adult friend about some of the areas that may be troublesome to you now.

ARE YOU READY FOR BAPTISM?

The following is shared with you as a guide to some of the things that may be important in helping you determine your readiness for baptism and church membership.

1. *You are ready for baptism . . .*
   . . . when you can say with certainty, "I am a follower of Christ."

Your commitment to Christ is the only condition that is really important to be ready for baptism. The first Christians experienced baptism immediately upon their conversion. For most of us who have grown up in the family of the church, recounting a definite time and place of "conversion" may be difficult, even impossible. Just because you cannot remember a specific time and place doesn't mean that you are not a Christian. Most of us have experienced "conversion" in many little steps of growth throughout our lives thus far. This kind of conversion is just as real as other experiences of conversion we hear about.

It all boils down to the awareness you have of Christ in your life now, the sincerity you feel in wanting to be His follower, and the willingness you feel within yourself to let Him control your life. It may also come in the awareness of a sinful nature which is pulling you away from Christ. No one is perfect in any of these things. We are always influenced by temptation. We often fail. But we cannot let our failures keep us from picking ourselves up again and again and recommitting ourselves to Christ. For persons who have grown up in the church and even been a Christian for some time, baptism can be an occasion for a very important recommitment, given publicly, which can strengthen our ties not only with Christ, but also with His church.

However, if you know that you have never made any commitment to be a follower of Christ, the time to make that commitment is now. You know the truth about Christ; you have been taught the meaning of finding new life in Him. To begin that life you might say, "Christ, I need to get on a new and better track in my life. I believe that You want to help me find a better way to live. I believe that You will help me stay on that track. If I do stray from it, I believe that You won't give up on me and will help me return to the way You want me to live. Walk with me in a brand new way, starting today, so that tomorrow will be different from yesterday."

2. *You are ready for baptism . . .*
    . . . when you can say, "I know that God is active in this world."

There have been people (called Deists) who have believed that God exists, but that He has gone off on vacation somewhere. They believe that He wound up the clock of the universe long ago and is now just waiting for it to tick itself out.

Christians cannot accept this notion about God.

They see Him at work in many ways: in people's lives that are changed; in nature and its wonders; in the history of nations and governments; but most important, they sense that God has an active purpose for their own lives.

Believing that God exists is not enough. We must also believe that He is active in the world, especially through the lives of Christians. Do you sense that God is (or wants to be) active in your life? In the lives of your friends? Is there awareness of the Holy Spirit as a source of power and guidance? Do you think that God wants to show His activity and intentions for your life through your baptism?

3. *You are ready for baptism . . .*

   . . . when you can say, "I know that God through Christ has accepted me. I am beginning to accept myself for what I am—a person who has something to share with others. I am beginning to see that others are accepting me for who I am."

Jesus said that "we must love our neighbors *as we love ourselves.*" Does loving yourself sound unchristian? It is not. In fact, it is the very foundation of many things: making a success of your life, making decisions about the future with confidence, feeling good about yourself and your relationships.

Loving yourself does not mean that you disregard others. Just the opposite occurs. Loving yourself makes it possible for you to love others. All of us have feelings of inferiority at times. Especially during the high school and college years we are often extremely self-conscious and aware of how others see us.

If you have serious questions about whether you "like yourself" this can make you feel less than ready for an experience such as baptism. Maybe you should talk to the pastor or another trusted adult about this. Maybe a good friend can help too, but choose that friend wisely, for he or she needs to be a sympathetic listener who you think will understand you.

4. *You are ready for baptism . . .*

> *. . . when you can say, "My relationships with the important people in my life are improving, or at least not getting any worse."*

Who are the important people in your life now? Parents will always be important people. Your relationship with them is changing and periods of change often bring stress and difficulties, even misunderstanding. You and your parents are adjusting to new understandings of each other. This often makes it hard on everyone. The conflicts you are experiencing are more normal than you may think. If you are not experiencing many conflicts with your parents you can feel fortunate because that probably means your communication with each other has been good and helped you all to work through your changing relationship in a peaceful, positive way. But if something is really wrong in your relationship with your parents, this can contribute to a feeling that you are not ready for baptism. It doesn't necessarily mean that you are not actually ready, but it may make you feel that way. It is something you need to talk over with your pastor or a trusted friend. Maybe you even need to approach your parents about it.

Friends, including those of the opposite sex, are also important people to whom you relate. Good relationships with your friends help you to feel good about yourself. There is security in friendships. We all need friends for support and companionship. If you feel unsure about your friends or if you feel that they are taking you in directions that do not follow a Christian lifestyle these are things that can affect your feelings of readiness for baptism. Again, talking it through with your pastor, your parents, or an understanding friend can help a lot.

Summary:

Life between the ages of sixteen and twenty-one is full of many decisions that help set the course of later life. Probably at no other time in your life will you be facing so many important decisions at the same time. It is a great age to be, but it is full of uncertainties and questions. You may long for the "old days" when life seemed simpler or fantasize about an adulthood in which you think that all the important decisions will be behind you. Actually, as we get older we do not have fewer important decisions to make, only the nature of the decisions change. *Adulthood means facing up to decisions* and learning how to make the right ones.

Among all the important decisions you must face now is the decision of whether to be baptized and assume full church membership, when to take this step, and how it should be done so that it can be an experience that is uniquely yours. If, after reading this paper, you feel you have gained a deeper understanding of yourself and your readiness for baptism, follow through by contacting the pastor to discuss your feelings further and to set a date for your baptism.

The fellowship of the church needs you. Jesus Christ wants you to witness to your faith in baptism. You also need the experience of baptism to help you continue your growth as a follower of Christ.

BIBLIOGRAPHY

Affirming Our Faith in Word and Deed. Scottdale, Pa.: Mennonite Publishing House, 1978.

Armour, Rollin S. *Anabaptist Baptism.* Scottdale, Pa.: Herald Press, 1966.

Beachy, Alvin J. *Worship as Celebration of Covenant and Incarnation.* Newton, Kansas: Faith and Life Press, 1968.

Driver, John. *Community and Commitment.* Scottdale, Pa.: Herald Press, 1976.

Enns, Herman. *This We Believe: Leader's Guide.* Newton, Kansas: Faith and Life Press, 1969.

Interpreter's Dictionary of the Bible. New York: Abingdon Press, 1962. Vol. A-D, "Baptism."

Jeschke, Marlin. *Discipling the Brother.* Scottdale, Pa.: Herald Press, 1972.

Jewett, Paul K. *Infant Baptism and the Covenant of Grace.* Grand Rapids: William B. Eerdmans, 1978.

Kehler, Larry. *Focus on Faith.* Newton, Kansas: Faith and Life Press, 1978.

Martin, Ernest D. *Preparing for Church Membership.* Scottdale, Pa.: Mennonite Publishing House, 1971.

Beasley-Murray, G. R. *Baptism in the New Testament.* Grand Rapids: William B. Eerdmans, 1973.

———. *The Story and Witness of the Christian Way.* Scottdale, Pa.: Mennonite Publishing House, 1971.

Mennonite Encyclopedia. Scottdale, Pa.: Mennonite Publishing House, 1955. Especially articles
"Admission into the Church," "Baptism," "Infant Baptism."

Mennonite Hymnal, The. Scottdale, Pa.: Herald
Press and Newton, Kansas: Faith and Life Press,
1969.

Miller, John W. *The Christian Way.* Scottdale, Pa.:
Herald Press, 1969.

Poettcker, Henry. *A Study on Baptism.* Newton,
Kansas: Faith and Life Press, 1963.

Schaller, Lyle E. *Assimilating New Members.*
Nashville: Abingdon, 1978.

Wainright, Geoffrey. *Christian Initiation.* Rich-
mond: John Knox Press, 1969.

Waltner, James H. *This We Believe.* Newton,
Kansas: Faith and Life Press, 1968.

Wenger, J. C. (ed.) *The Complete Writings of
Menno Simons.* Scottdale, Pa.: Herald Press,
1956.

Wenger, John Paul. *Because God Loves.* Scottdale,
Pa.: Herald Press, 1976.

Westerhoff, John H. III. *Will Our Children Have
Faith?* New York: The Seabury Press, 1976.

White, R. E. O. *The Biblical Doctrine of Initiation.*
Grand Rapids: William B. Eerdmans, 1960.